Bilingual Complex:
Collection of Essays and Notes Featuring English Haiku

バイリンガル・コンプレックス

Kyoko Norma Nozaki

野﨑　京子

Contents

Preface

Bilingualism is believed to help prevent or delay dementia. I don't know how valid and scientifically proven the information is but I just hope it is as I am equally comfortable in Japanese and English. Also, now that I am in the last year of my seventies, becoming eighty is like stepping into an unknown territory.

I have always been interested in haiku, but was kind of hesitant to join any Japanese haiku groups, as they seemed so cliquish. It led me to turn to English haiku as I also wanted to stay in touch with the language. Then, a friend of mine, who was a visiting professor from the Philippines in English literature, mentioned an English haiku group, Hailstone, led by a British haiku poet, Stephen Gill. I joined the group in 2011, the year I retired from a private university in Kyoto after teaching there for 33 years.

It has been my source of intellectual stimulus along with my active participation in academic study groups.

I have published many academic papers and some of my English haiku were included in compilations by Hailstone, but this book is my first work of haiku-inspired essays as a single author.

Over the years, I have accumulated English haiku and essays which were products of my haiku excursions, travels as well as my everyday life. They are like souvenir photos that trigger my recollection of the memorable moments.

Through these haiku essays, I hope to share with the readers some of the unforgettable sceneries I have experienced.

March, 2019
Kyoko Norma Nozaki
野崎　京子

Ⅰ.

Haibun/Essays Featuring English Haiku

Eternal Life

Through swaying veils
Curvaceous figures carved–
The Ancient wall

It was in October 2015 that my husband and I went to Angkor Wat, Cambodia with our daughter and a grandson. She has been stationed in Bangkok for a few years, and during our stay there she arranged our trip to the ruins near Siem Reap, about a one-hour flight from Bangkok. I knew it was a UNESCO World Heritage Site, but until then, I had not known exactly where it was located.

We saw many relief carvings on massive stone walls. What impressed me was how sensual and lifelike the female figures were depicted. Among them, the story of the Naga, the snake goddess, is quite thought-provoking. In myths, legends, scripture and folklore, the Naga are comprised of all kinds of serpentine beings in Cambodian culture and represent eternal life.

It was particularly interesting to me that the founder of the Bayon Temple, Jayavarman VII, was romantically linked with the mystic creature.

When I learned that Mishima Yukio（三島由紀夫）was inspired to write his last play, *The Terrace of the Leper King*（『ライ病王のテラス』）upon his visit on October 25th 1965, I felt a kind of fate, as my visit there was exactly 50 years after his.

In the play, as the king physically deteriorates with the progression of his disease, the only woman who willingly beds with him is the immortal Naga.

The play was a consequence of Mishima's research trip to Bangkok for his well-known novel *The Temple of Dawn*（『暁の寺』）. It is said that when he saw a statue of Jayavarman, who was rumored to suffer from leprosy, Mishima's artistic imagination sprung up to tell the tragic life of this young, ambitious and handsome king. Because of leprosy, the king's youthful body gradually deteriorates while the temple is being built to its perfect completion. The irony is that the frailty of human flesh is replaced by the grandeur of the man-made structure, the Bayon Temple in Angkor Wat.

Mishima was so passionate about the play that it took him four years to complete the work. It was a tragic twist of fate that he and his comrade committed suicide in public in 1975, only a year after the first performance of the play was staged. Despite receiving excellent reviews, it had not been performed again on stage until quite recently in Tokyo, apparently because the word 'leprosy' had been considered politically incorrect.

The reason I was fascinated with the story of the king was its theme: fatal disease and aging. It is a well-known fact that Mishima was obsessed with keeping his body in shape, as he feared aging and dreaded the ugliness of old age. It seems he longed for eternal youth and did not care about longevity. He killed himself at the age of 45.

I believe the curvaceous bodies carved on the walls symbolize his adoration for perpetual beauty and incarnation of life. How can human beings attain such a dream? The only solution to the impossibility that historical people in power have sought after was reproducing oneself, that is, giving birth to next generation. So what if one is infertile and cannot reproduce, particularly if one is expected to have an heir to a kingdom?

Once I happened to visit the tomb of the Empress Shoken（昭憲皇后）, wife of the Emperor Meiji（明治天皇）. She did not bear him any children, but he had many other wives and children. When I saw a number of baby seedlings, shoots, on her tomb grounds, I could not help thinking about her caged life in feudalistic Japan and composed the following haiku.

Pine seedlings
Sprouting here and there–
The childless empress

Temple of Dawn

Temple of Dawn
Silhouetted in the twilight,
Viewed from a once-royal villa
Not a mid-summer night's dream

On Aug. 29, 2018 we visited Bangkok's Wat Arun, Wat Pho and the Grand Palace because despite his many visits to Thailand, my husband Mitch had never visited these must-see tourist spots.

My daughter managed to get a reservation at the

renowned Chakrabongse Villa named after the grandson of King Chulalongkan, which had been a royal villa until 1920's. We enjoyed the view of the Wat Arun from the balcony.

This is the temple that inspired Mishima Yukio to write his novel, *Temple of Dawn.* The protagonist of the novel, who is said to be Mishima himself, was inspired to go to India in order to find out why Buddhism developed more outside its birth country. We know Hinduism is the dominant religion in India.

I noticed Hindu influences on the sculptures and carvings, although Buddhism has penetrated into the everyday life of ordinary people. We often see people making offerings to Buddhist monks on streets. Buddhist monks are highly respected and we, especially women and foreigners, are not supposed to approach and talk to them in casual way.

Once I made a mistake by asking a monk for directions, which was pointed out by my 9-year old grandson. He said I was "rude" in starting to talk to him. It showed how much they are revered in the country.

Lotus Garden

Over the Red Lotus Pond
Drone chasing our boat
For picture taking

During our two-week stay in Thailand, August 2018, we took a day trip to the Red Lotus Garden about an hour drive from Bangkok.

It was very pastoral as the pond was full of beautiful bright pink lotus and other aquatic plants and birds. What I thought interesting was the use of drone to take bird-eye pictures of the visitors.

I think it is a fantastic idea as it is difficult to take our pictures while on board. It flew above us and zoroed in and out from different directions. The photos were ready when we got off the boat. There were more than 70 pictures of our family that we could choose from and the entire set was selling for 300 Thai Baht (about 10 US$). We chose the latter and as soon as we paid our 300 THB, 70 photos were immediately transferred to our smartphones.

It is amazing to see how high-tech some things are in Thailand while they are still developing in other ways.

Crackling Firewood

My turn to toll the temple bell
The New Year begins–
Firewood crackling

During the past several years we have been going to Myomanji（妙満寺）, a Buddhist temple, walking-distance from our house on December 31st to ring in the New Year after eating *toshikoshi soba*（年越しそば）, a traditional soba dish. It is usually around half an hour before midnight when we arrive at the temple. We queue up to ring the bell（除夜の鐘）, as it is believed that the ringing of bells can rid our sins of the year. *Amazake*（甘酒）, fermented mild sake, are offered to the temple visitors. This non-alcoholic sweet sake is seasoned with grated ginger, which warms up the body temperature and is good for curing colds and developing immunity to all sorts of diseases.

The bonus is a Japanese sweet served with a bowl of *matcha* tea（抹茶）in a tatami room with a view of a zen garden. The ritual is complete with writing your

New Year's wish on a small wooden plaque called *ema* (絵馬), depicting that year's zodiac sign.

This year it was only my husband and myself. Last year we began the New Year with one of my daughters' family with their two pet dogs.

The year before, we went in a big group of ten: both daughters with their families and a friend. On the way back, we played tag and were surprised to find how much our grandchildren had grown. Boy, were they fast and agile!

Looking back, there was a year that had quite a snowfall, so we could enjoy the snow-covered garden while savoring the sweet and *matcha.*

Each year, we wish for our health and peaceful society. This year's visit to the temple was particularly significant as we approach the end of the *Heisei Era* (平成) which lasted for 30 years without any war.

The bonfire is for burning the *ema* from the previous year. It was the year of the dog, an animal known to be loyal and to render devoted service to his/her master. 2019 is the year of the wild boar, symbol of strong will and determination.

I saw people's faces brighten up with the light of the bonfire, and perhaps with a sense of expectation for the new era.

Crackling firewood–
Having prayed for New Year luck
Faces glow

First Snow

January 3rd–
Promising prosperity,
A flurry of snow

I recently learned that '*osagari*', which usually means 'hand-me-downs', is used in haiku to imply 'fertility.' The Chinese characters in this case are （御降り）, which mean 'honorable fall' and is different from the common use of 'osagari' （お下がり）.

I am just glad that the chaotic period between the end of the year and early into the New Year is almost over. How I long to be away from all this hustle and bustle and dream of traveling to an exotic place abroad!

Many years have gone by spending this time of the year, preparing festive New Year dishes, decorating the front door with ornamental straw and fulfilling other protocols. Perhaps I should be thankful for being able to perform these rituals in the past years. However, I cannot help feeling that this is not what I really wanted and recall a famous poem composed by Onono Komachi （小野小町）, a poetess renowned for her beauty from

Heian period (平安時代).

Colors of cherry blossoms fade
in vain,
My fruitless years went by
while gazing them

花の色はうつりにけりないたずらに
わが身世にふるながめせしまに

Symphony Fantastic

Once a boisterous young conductor,
Referred to as a samurai with a baton–
A frail-looking old man now

It was in the early 1960's, I met a young conductor, Seiji Ozawa（小澤征爾）backstage at the San Francisco Symphony Hall after he conducted the French composer (Berlioz)'s masterpiece. I was an undergraduate student at University of California, Berkeley and a group of Japanese students and scholars were invited to visit the budding conductor, whose talent was recognized by Herbert von Karajan, the world-famous German artist.

The San Francisco Chronicle reported his debut as a young samurai, as he passionately conducted the orchestra, swaying his baton as if it was his sword. I still remember the front-page picture of his charismatic appearance on the stage: lion-mane hair dancing as he moved his baton in all directions. Backstage, he greeted us warmly, accompanied by his pianist wife at the time.

Later, he and his family moved to Boston and he became a popular conductor at the Tanglewood summer concert for many years. It was in 1986 that I went to one of those concerts, and found his performance more mature and sophisticated, almost mellow, compared to the one almost 20 years earlier.

I understand Symphony Fantastic has been his favorite and wonder if it is because of the life of Berlioz or his music. Is life just a dream or fantasy?

Dazaifu

Iris hue
in a palette of the shrine pond–
legacy of Flying Plum tree behind

My husband and I traveled to Dazaifu, Fukuoka（福岡県太宰府）immediately after attending a conference held in the same prefecture in June, 2018. It is a shrine built over the grave of Sugawara Michizane（菅原道真）a tragic government officer exiled to Kyushu because of a 10th century political scandal. Having been a celebrated scholar then, he was hailed as the God of literature and calligraphy, and even now, students taking entrance exams of all kinds flock to his shrines all over Japan.

There are many anecdotes about him often associated with poems, but the most famous one is *tobiume*（飛梅）the flying plum tree. According to legend, upon his departure from Kyoto for a life in exile, he wrote,

When the east wind blows
Oh plum blossoms
Let it send your fragrance,
Do not forget the spring,
though your master is gone

東風吹かば　にほひをこせよ梅の花
主なしとて春な忘れそ

This particular tree yearned so much for him that, uprooting itself, it flew to reunite with him in Dazaifu, and the plum tree, which still blooms every year, has been enshrined in the precinct.

It is my high school's tradition to have a farewell picnic there every year at the end of February, as March is the last month of the academic year in Japan. I looked at the familiar site in a melancholic mood. The irony is that our high school is a Methodist affiliated school, but no one seemed to question it.

Instead of plum, I enjoyed various kinds of iris in the shrine garden on the day the rainy season was declared in Kyushu.

Acorns

Acorns scattered
all over the herb garden–
Immune from the nuclear plant?

Our English haiku group travelled to the Takahama and Ōi（高浜と大飯）district of Wakasa Bay, Fukui Prefecture（福井県若狭湾）, staying overnight at a comfortable lodge in mid November, 2017. There were nine of us, and in the autumn showers, for a good five hours the six men took a rigorous hike to Aobayama（青葉山）. We three women had a relaxing afternoon in the herb garden at the base of the mountain.

In the midst of trees and herbs, I found acorns laying all over on the ground, along with fallen pine needles. I realized that we were not too far away from the Ōi nuclear plant（大飯原発）. It was on March 11, 2011 that the Great East Japan Earthquake（東日本大震災）struck, causing nuclear leakages in Fukushima Prefecture（福島県）. While there is a considerable distance between the two nuclear plants, I could not help being apprehensive about what might happen in other operating plants.

Was the vegetation not exposed to the radiation? Living in Kyoto and getting our water from Lake Biwa (琵琶湖), are we safe from contamination?

Ten-year-old Boy

His head on my lap,
No space for stretched out legs
in the back seat—
A baby, ten years ago

My ten-year-old grandson, Jules Kosuke（光輔）, asked me if I have a brother or sister. Since he is an only child while many of his friends have siblings, it could be just a simple curiosity. I answered, "I had a big brother, but he died when he was a child, so I grew up thinking I was an only child."

Come to think of it, my brother was nearly the same age as my grandson now and I told him his tragic death as following, adapted from the Prologue in my paper, "Four Generations of Japanese American Women in the Work of Janice Mirikitani," (1998).

It was a warm day in May 1946 in a small town in Japan. A boy was about to walk to a station to meet his father, who was the only one he could talk to in English. The boy, Hiroshi（博）Barbi, was a Japanese boy, but could not speak Japanese. He had been in the fourth grade at a school in a relocation center in Utah, when his parents decided to go back to their ancestral home in Fukuoka, Japan. It had been nearly five months since they returned. His sister, Kyoko（京子）Norma, and Hiroshi started school in April. Being in the first grade, Kyoko did not have any problems in adjusting to Japanese culture and language, in contrast to Hiroshi. His language, manner and the way he dressed made him self-conscious and that prevented him from making friends easily with local boys.

Returnee, the word sounds modern–
Hidden behind,
Loneliness and longing for companion

Hence it became his daily habit to meet his father, who was working with the American occupation army as an interpreter, at a train station. The father loved talking to his only son, who was born in California on Abraham Lincoln's birthday. Hiroshi was given one character "博" from what the president was often referred to, 'philanthropist,'（博愛主義者）. The father was hoping Hiroshi would go to Harvard or Princeton University and become a doctor someday. Hiroshi's grandfather had immigrated to the U.S.A. in the beginning of the 20th century and came back to Japan at the age of 61. It was his house that Hiroshi's family was staying in.

As he started to walk toward the station, he met one of his classmates and decided to get a ride on a horse-drawn wagon, heading for the direction. Unfortunately, the boys did not ask the driver's permission and the wagon was full of logs. When it arrived in front of the station, Hiroshi tried to jump off from the wagon as his friend did. But his suspenders got caught in one of the wheels and he was pulled under the wagon. When his parents rushed to the site, there was nothing they could do as the heavy load had crushed the boy's internal organs. His sister, Kyoko, heard the mother muttering, "We came back to Japan to have our only son killed . . ."

This is how I lost my brother in 1946.

Hiroshi and Kyoko

Jules Kosuke as Wally

Rituals for Growing Up

Every Christmas, I have been writing a greeting letter which is more like a newsletter of our family. The oldest I have kept in my computer file is 2008（平成 20 年）, a year before our grandson was born. There is a photo of our then only grandchild, Kyoka（京佳）

dressed in kimono taken on her 7-5-3 celebration（七五三）. It is a joyful occasion to commemorate when a child comes to the respective age. (It started in ancient times, when the rate of infant mortality was so high, that being alive at the age of 3 was a great cause for celebration.) We visited Kamigamo Shrine（上賀茂神社）, where she also had a newborn ceremony three years earlier.

Since her birth, she has been a joy to her parents, Kazu and Aoi, who had waited almost 15 years for the birth of their only child. Mitch, a proud grandfather, had been a willing and devoted babysitter to relieve Aoi when she was busy with work.

Ever since Kyoka started her first year at Doshisha International Academy (DIA) elementary school, he had been regularly staying overnight at their house to look after her.

The practice continued until she entered junior high school in the spring of 2018, and at the same time, her family moved back to Osaka. Now that, she is a junior high school student, she is old enough to take care of herself, such as commuting to school, going to extra-curricular activities, and being at home with no help from a care taker.

Her grandfather is happy that she grew up to this age, no longer needing his help and yet nostalgically recalls the precious six years he looked after her.

As if to signify her coming of age, her family and relatives had the *Jusan (13)-mairi* celebration.

Jyusan-mairi is a temple visit made by 13-year old boys and girls with their parents, to give thanks for their coming of age. It is a folk custom believed to have originated in Kyoto, but now a common ceremony all over Japan.

Kyoto, which had been the national capital for over 1200 years, still has customs, holidays and folklore for maintaining tradition and legacy. Following customs, such as 7-5-3 and *Jyusan-Mairi,* are important practices.

Our grandson, Jules Kosuke, has never lived in Japan, but we have managed to celebrate both his 3rd and 5th year in a traditional way in Kamigamo Shrine. I cannot believe that it will be his turn to celebrate Jusan

-mairi in just two years-time. We very much look forward to seeing him again in *hakama.*

Among many protocols for the celebration for 13 year-olds in Kyoto, probably the most important one is never to look back while walking on the Togetsu Bridge（渡月橋）in Arashiyama（嵐山）. Like many other customs, we no longer know the reason. I only assume that it implies that youth should never look back but move forward.

Kyoka's mother decided to have the celebration in November, about a month before her 13th birthday. Both mother and the daughter wore beautiful kimono. It was a glorious autumn day with colored maples all over.

Looking at the photos taken on the day, I realize my granddaughter has certainly grown up to be a young lady. At the same time, history and tradition, which require certain rituals and protocols, make sense, though at times they seem cumbersome and time-consuming.

Ⅱ.

Research Notes Featuring English Haiku

Asian Faces

On October 30, 2018, I decided to fly to Berkeley, California where I completed my undergraduate studies, as I had some personal matters to take care of. I also went to see a cousin in San Jose, where I attended a high school in 1958, exactly 60 years ago. At that time, San Jose was just a sleepy agricultural town, full of fruit orchards. Now it has turned into an IT center, known as the Silicon Valley.

A valley of orchards
Now, a vast tech center
Dream on California

Although many things have changed in the past few decades in California, one thing that has not changed is the increasing Asian population, next to the largest ethnic minority, Hispanics, in the Golden State.

However, unlike most Asian decent Americans, some Hispanics and Latinos claim and register themselves as racially "white" and are sometimes statistically included in the white population.

When we talk about the percentages of minority residents, California has always had the largest number of Asians in the country, whereas other states have relatively few Asians, making them a minority of minorities. (Asian Americans including multiracial Americans identifying as partially Asian, are only 5.6% of the total American population, whereas in California, 14.7%)

Here is an episode that illustrates the phenomenon.

In September, I went to see the movie, "*Crazy Rich Asians,*" based on the best-selling book of the same title by Kevin Kwan who stated that his intention in writing the novel was to "introduce a contemporary Asia to the North American audience." An American friend of mine whom I went to see the film with noticed that the Japanese title of the movie was "Crazy Rich" (「クレイジー・リッチ」) without the mention of "Asians."

According to a Japanese university professor friend of mine who grew up in the US, "the people who come up with film titles in Japanese have no regard for original titles or grammar," and "they left out "Asians" because Japanese are Asians, too." She also pointed out that the film has a universal appeal to a wider audience beyond ethnicity and location. Her friend in the Mid-West has a *hapa* (a person who is partially of Asian or Pacific Islander descent) son, who went to see the film three times: once with his parents, then with his friends, and then with his high school's Asian American club. I felt his excitement, as the film's Asian characters were humanly portrayed, and it had been 25 years since an all Asian cast American film, "The Joy Luck Club," was produced.

Some demographic scholars are predicting that Asians would become the largest ethnic group in the US by 2050, surpassing Hispanic group. Looking at the ever-growing number of Asian tourists in Higashiyama, a sightseeing area in Kyoto, I have a feeling that they may be right. We will see.

Note on Expats

"The Kansai area in Japan was hit by a damaging earthquake (mag. 5.5) on June 18, 2018 and had a monsoon-like rainstorm which caused floods in early July", as our haiku group's website reported.

This unusual weather forced many official plans and events to be cancelled, including many of my study group meetings. At the same time, Japan was gripped by an intense heat wave throughout the summer that dreaded many tourists in Kyoto, especially when the thermometer rose to 40°C on July 18. Ten days later, as if to cool things down, a typhoon hit the country causing heartbreaking disaster.

Helicopter hovering over,
people on a rooftop–
Never-ending rain

One month later my husband and I took off from Kansai Airport to spend two weeks in Bangkok. For the first time, we felt that Thailand was cooler than Japan. According to a guidebook, May to October in Thailand is fairly comfortable as daily showers cool down the temperature.

I composed the following haiku in English first then Japanese came later.

Red lotus floating–
Paradise or
Chaos on the earth
赤睡蓮　浮かぶ地上の楽園は　混沌の世か

Sounds like the American Southern drawl–
Thai echo
In my eardrum
南部なまりのごと聞こえ
鼓膜にタイ語の響き

White expats merging and mixing
In the Asian neighbor–
Glimpse of the near future
近未来，タイに流れ入る　異国人《トツクニビト》

During our numerous visits to Bangkok, where our daughter has been living since 2013, we have met many "expats" (expatriates) through my grandson's friends. I have to explain what "expats" are to Japanese people, as the concept of leaving one's home country and residing in another country is not common among Japanese.

Our grandson was born in Paris (France) and moved to Hong Kong at the age of two and then to Bangkok at the age of four. Most of his friends are multinational and multilingual expat kids. It is not an exaggeration to say that he has friends "all over the world" as many of his friends are now living in places such as Singapore, South Africa, Dubai, Switzerland, Kenya after leaving their expat lives in Bangkok.

His best friend Louis, a French boy who was born in Hong Kong and raised in Bangkok, moved to La Reunion, a French island in the Indian Ocean last year, much to our grandson's dismay. However the two boys are still very much in contact, thanks to modern communication technologies and also to Louis' family's generous hospitality. Our grandson stayed with them for two weeks at their new home in La Reunion last year and he will be spending three weeks at their holiday house in South of Italy this summer. It is quite fascinating to see our grandson, at such a young age, exposed to and easily adapt to cultures and places that I have never had the chance to acquaint.

Looking at the holiday pictures from La Reunion made me recall of a student who was studying at Kyoto Sangyo University in the early 2000's. Josephine was an African decent French girl from La Reunion and some Japanese students could not grasp the fact that France is a multi-racial/cultural country. In order to make my color-blind Japanese students aware of the fact, I invited her to speak in one of my culture study classes. My husband and I were studying French as a hobby at that time, so we also invited her to our house and learned about her native homeland.

Expat と呼ばれる Expatriate は、自分が生まれたり育った国以外で生活している人たちである。筆者が香港やバンコクで知り合った多くの欧米人はこれに該当する。筆者の10歳になる孫（男子）はフランスのパリで生まれ、2歳から香港、4歳からバンコクに住んでいて、香港時代からリセ・フランセと呼ばれるフランス政府の教育機関に通っている。リセ・フランセはフランス国外に住むフランス国籍の子どものフランス語教育を目的とした幼稚園から高校で世界中に500近くの学校がある。フランス人以外にも様々な国籍の子どもが通っており、知り合った孫の友人の多くがこのExpatカテゴリーに属している。

Note on Immigration

It was in September, 2014 that I visited Kobayashi Issa's (小林一茶 1763～1827) Memorial Museum in Shinano, Nagano（長野県信濃）.

I was immediately struck by the big board at the entrance, which bears his haiku,

今日からは日本の雁よ　楽に寝よ
（*Kyo kara wa Nihon no kariyo Rakuni neyo*）

It describes a conversation with a migratory goose, "From today, you are a Japanese goose, so relax and sleep in comfort." This made me think of Japanese immigrants, particularly of my grandparents.

My grandparents, both paternal and maternal, immigrated to Hawaii to work on a sugar plantation in the early twentieth century, more than 100 years ago.

My personal interest has led me to research the history of Japanese immigrants and I have interviewed many of them in their advanced age, but their memories were quite intact. I have also read many of their haiku which recorded their harsh immigrant life and their longing for their home country.

Mt. Fuji
the top appears over the cloud
Ultimate icon of nostalgia

I composed this haiku on my way to Tokyo on March 3, 2018. I had a good view of Mt. Fuji through a window of the bullet train (新幹線). I was attending a forum on Japanese Brazilian immigrants in Tokyo. Later, I felt empathy with them and thought of the cruel anti-immigrant act of President Trump, which has been upsetting the USA.

Diversity, one of the strengths of the USA, is now being threatened. However, when I look at a picture of Trump's cabinet members, in the Jan.10, 2019 issue of *Time,* I can't help admiring the new, "most diverse congress" we have ever had, and am optimistic about seeing change in the immigration policy.

Life of a *Kibei Nisei* Woman

She was born on July 4th, 1916, in Oxnard, California, but raised in Fukuoka, Japan from the age of six. Her Japanese name means “victory branch,（勝枝）” as if to commemorate American Independence Day in the country of birth. She was a nursing student when she met and married Storm Tanigawa, a Nisei（second generation 二世）from California.

Her younger sister, told me that it was love at first sight as she remembered her saying, “I am going to marry this guy! I am certain of that.” So at the age of 19, the oldest of four children, she was a determined and head-strong young woman and brave enough to marry a young man who was living in a country across the Pacific Ocean, far away from her family. Besides, “victory branch” also means “strong-minded” and “unyielding.”

In California, she gave birth to two children, Hiroshi and Kyoko, Yes, she is my mother, a *kibei*（帰米）, a Japanese American who was born in the U.S.A., but brought up in Japan.

Despite her years in the States, she had never

learned to speak English and was always more comfortable with Japanese language and life style. I remember how my husband's father described her when they met for the first time, "I kind of expected to see a sophisticated Nikkei woman, but she turned out to be a naïve country girl I felt comfortable with."

Like many other pre-war Nikkei women, she had led a harsh and turbulent life in two countries during the War.

Waves running high–
Aboard a transpacific boat,
Volition on a young face

1945 must had been the most difficult year for her. In February, my father was apprehended by FBI and sent to Bismarck, (North Dakota), leaving her in Tule Lake Camp with two small children.

It was not until Dec. 29th that year that she was reunited with her husband on board the USS Gordon as it set off for Japan.

Whenever I give a presentation about the Japanese American internment at conferences, I realize I can not speak much about a woman's point of view, probably because while my father was open about his camp experiences, my mother kept her silence.

His stories were supported by public documents I received from the National Archives and Record Administration (NARA アメリカ国立公文書館), Washington D.C. in 2006, but a file about my mother revealed very little. For example, mug shots of my father revealed his vital statistics including a full set of his fingerprints along with his height and weight, but there were none for my mother. According to an archivist, it is common practice not to document such information about housewives as their lives often remained within a house.

However, there are a few pictures of her taken at the camp, which, I believe, reflect her mental state then. One group photo shows her standing at the last row with her face half hidden (in front of the door). It was probably taken after a dress-making class, a rare hobby for her, but a pragmatic one as she did not allow herself the luxury of simple pleasures. She used to say having hobbies was a waste of time as they do not produce anything of use. She was quite opinionated, unlike women of her generation, and this ascetic attitude gave her an image of a strict mother.

She was only about 28 years old, stranded alone with two small children, not knowing why her husband was sent to a far-away federal camp in another state and if and when they would get reunited, all of which must have shaped her to become such a disciplinarian. The photo was taken in 1944～45 in front of a camp housing, which was covered with coal tar paper. It makes a striking contrast to a family portrait, taken earlier, in which she looks radiantly happy.

The symptoms of depression she started in her late 40s was most likely related to the trauma she experienced in her late 20s. She may never have recovered from the mental scars, and the final blow was the sudden death of my brother, Hiroshi, within five months of our arrival back in Japan. The tragedy was described in my essay, "Ten-year-old Boy," earlier in this book.

There were a few years when she looked relatively happy, around 1990, when the redress（戦時補償）had been finalized and a check amounting to $20,000 was mailed to her from the U.S. government as a compensation（補償金）for Japanese American internment. The accompanying letter from the US President George Bush may have helped her feel that her hardship was finally acknowledged.

THE WHITE HOUSE
WASHINGTON

A monetary sum and words alone cannot restore lost years or erase painful memories; neither can they fully convey our Nation's resolve to rectify injustice and to uphold the rights of individuals. We can never fully right the wrongs of the past. But we can take a clear stand for justice and recognize that serious injustices were done to Japanese Americans during World War II.

In enacting a law calling for restitution and offering a sincere apology, your fellow Americans have, in a very real sense, renewed their traditional commitment to the ideals of freedom, equality, and justice. You and your family have our best wishes for the future.

Sincerely,

GEORGE BUSH
PRESIDENT OF THE UNITED STATES

OCTOBER 1990

“A monetary sum and words alone cannot restore lost years or erase painful memories; . . . . But we can take a clear stand for justice and recognize that serious injustices were done to Japanese Americans during World War II.”

In her 70s, she developed a kidney failure and went through dialysis every other day for almost eight years, until she passed away at the age of 82. However, she seemed to accept her fate at the end.

Red gerbera
My mother’s favorite
Revived with a stem broken

My Nisei Father, Major League Baseball, and Marilyn Monroe

As one of the academic newsletter editors was reading my father's life story in my book *Internment and Identity Shift*（『強制収容とアイデンティティ・シフト』）, he asked me if I could write about my father's hobby in conjunction with my research on Japanese Americans. My father used to tell me that he has no hobby, but looking back, I could think of several pastimes he used to enjoy.

My father, Tsutomu Storm Tanigawa（谷川 力ストーム）, was born in Watsonville, California on June 1st, 1909.

The fog lifts up in Golden State,
Sunny California–
Dream of my immigrant grandfather

My paternal grandparents, Montaro and Tsumo（紋太郎とツモ）, immigrated to California via Hawaii, arriving in San Francisco just a few days before the

1906 earthquake.

My father was born the second son and grew up with his big brother Kazuo（一夫）in a carefree environment. Considering the unstable political and diplomatic relationship between Japan and the United States at that time, I could not help assuming that the circumstances were rather grim, yet my father insisted that there was no racial or ethnic discrimination from local residents who were mainly Germans, Italians and Portuguese. (Amazingly, he remembered many of the neighborhood children's names, like Pete and Pearl, and the games they used to play, like shooting BB guns.)

He always had positive and optimistic characteristics of an "all-American boy," which might have been cultivated in such a multi-ethnic and friendly environment. He had a special attachment to American cars by such makers as Ford and Chevrolet, because those were the first cars he drove as a teenager. His favorite food remained steak and potatoes, and he loved Hollywood movies, which became his work.

My father was in his early 30s and my mother was in her mid 20s when my parents were forcefully relocated to the internment camps for Japanese Americans living on the West Coast. They were an ordinary young couple with two children. Before the evacuation, they owned their own strawberry farm next to the ones owned by his brother's and sister's families. With help from Mexican and Filipino farm hands, they had a busy but promising and fulfilling life. In addition to managing the farm, my father enrolled himself in University of California evening courses, which did not give him any spare time for hobbies.

Abandoning ripened strawberries unpicked,
Aroma of fruit fills the field–
To a camp with a broken promise

During harvest time, he had to work nearly 20 hours a day picking ripened strawberries, and at night he tied a flashlight around his head to continue the work. Ironically, it was his time at the internment camp that gave him the opportunity to pursue new interests for the first time since his childhood.

During his ten months in Bismarck, North Dakota, alone and away from us, he sent my brother and me wooden pencil boxes with a drawing on the lid. I remember mine had a little girl with "Kyoko Norma" written on a blackboard, and a little white puppy alongside her. I vaguely recall that my brother's had an illustration of a boy in a baseball uniform with a glove and a bat. The surface was shiny so my father must have varnished the boxes. Unfortunately they were lost over the years, though I fondly remember the rounded and smoothed corners of our pencil cases.

The Fort Lincoln camp in Bismarck had better facilities than the War Relocation Authority camps (WRA 戦時転住局). He told us he had spent quite a long time in a woodworking factory, where some of his fellow carpenter inmates taught him how to craft wood. He must have made those pencil boxes himself thinking of us and sent them together with chocolate he bought at the canteen there.

At Bismarck camp, movies were shown almost every night and he went to watch them at the camp theater twice a week. It was the main source of entertainment for the inmates and I am sure my father was not the only one who fell in love with the lavish world presented by Hollywood. After the war, my father contributed in promoting Hollywood movies in Japan by managing an American film distribution company in Kyushu.

In the 1940's, baseball was probably the most

popular sport in the US and it was no different inside the internment camps. Each block had at least one baseball team. A group photo of a Little League baseball team taken at the Tule Lake Camp in 1945 shows my brother Hiroshi, then 8 years old, the youngest of the team. When the photo was taken, my father was away from us, interned alone in Fort Lincoln Enemy Alien Camp（敵性外国人抑留所）in North Dakota.

Looking back upon those days, he told me later in his life that he regretted not being able to play catch and watch Hiroshi play in the game. It was not common for my optimistic father to express regrets, but there was a good reason for him saying that. After the 10-month separation, our family was reunited on board the SS Gordon, which left Port Portland, Oregon for Japan

on December 29th, 1945. Five months after our arrival in Japan, my brother Hiroshi died in an accident in May, 1946. His funeral photo was copied and enlarged from the Little League baseball group picture. (2nd row, 2nd from the right.)

In the 1950's, my father was working as the general manager of the Kyushu branch of the American Motion Picture Distribution Company. It was through his work that my father and I had a chance to meet Joe DiMaggio, the American Major Leaguer, and Marilyn Monroe, during their honeymoon in February, 1954. He was asked to welcome the actress, who was going to be entertaining the American troops in Korea. My father asked me "Would you like to meet Marilyn Monroe?" The company prepared a bouquet of flowers for me to present to her, and the local newspaper published an article of the visit at that time.

When we walked into their suite in Hakata International Hotel（博多国際ホテル）, Joe was in the living room, and then after a few minutes, Marilyn came out from the bedroom. I remember her creamy white complexion, and her tight black skirt, which accentuated her waist. Even though her lipstick was smudged, I

thought she was beautiful. She smiled at me and gave me an autographed photo with the message, "To Norma," which is my middle name as well as her real first name. This of course is not a coincidence. My father was a fan of Marilyn Monroe.

This happy event symbolizes, to me, my father's fond affection towards two things that are truly American: baseball and Hollywood, which he probably cultivated during his internment in the Bismarck camp.

As I finished writing this draft and returned from

Hong Kong, a check from the Bank of America was delivered to me in Japan. It was a check signed by my father. It had been an annual event for him to write a check to mail order See's Candies for his friends and relatives for the holiday season, which continued until 2011, when he passed away at the age of 101. I miss this ritual and the box of See's chocolates, another thing American that my father was truly fond of.

A box of chocolate
Christmas gift by my Nisei father
Shipped from California

Ⅲ.

English Haiku

2011

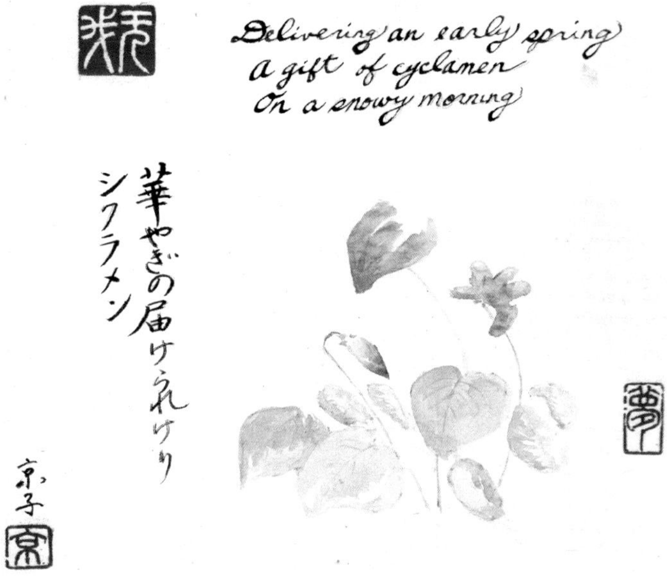

1) *Delivering an early spring*
A gift of cyclamen
On a snowy morning

(*Tenkoku*（篆刻）Exhibition,
North Bunka Hall, Kyoto, Dec.)

2013～2014

2) *Munching a white sausage*
In a crowded tavern–
Oktoberfest is near

(Munich, Oct., 2013)

3) *Shuffling on a polished stage,*
My father-in-law revived
Behind a mask of Noh-player

(Kyoto, Jan., 2014)

4) *Messages from the past*
Come back to me–
fragile yet hard

(San Francisco, Feb.)

5) *A blooming colonnade—*
Along the Takano River
Assailed by memories

(Kyoto, April)

6) *My kitchen garden*
So lush and green—
Vegetables shout their joy

(July)

7) *Autumn canvas—*
Eggplant's dusky purple
Persimmon's yellow-brown

(Sept.)

8) *A crust of cauliflower*
from our kitchen garden
Casserole dish tonight

(Oct.)

9) *Gleam*
Of black polished pillars–
The entertainment house

(Shimabara, Kyoto, Dec.)

10) *Lattice and curves–*
Optical illusion
On a sliding paper door

(same as above)

11) *Cool breeze from flashing water*
Venders' boats in floating market
(Bangkok, Dec.)

2015～2016

12) *Basking in*
Tropical aroma–
New Year's Eve
(Back from Bangkok, Jan., 2015)

13) *Vermillion gates in line*
Though cliché and trite–
Our first shrine visit of the year
(Fushimi, Jan., 2016)

14) *Thousand Vermillion Gates*
Taking my New Year's prayer–
jostling around the crowds

(same as above)

15) *A Single Camellia*
Lying on the ground
Caressing fern–
Life goes on

(Feb.～March)

16) *Temple garden–*
Beautiful, cold-hearted
Hydrangea

(Sanzen-in, June)

17) *Twilight silhouette*
of Mt. Fuji flashed past
Awaiting the rains

(Shizuoka, June)

18) *Childhood memories*
−shellfish gathering
from days long gone

(Tokyo, June)

2017〜2018

19) *Carp flying*
against the current
above the new leaves

(Shiga, May, 2017)

20) *Snow-covered runway–*
an Indian summer was waiting
at the other end

(Denver to Narita, Oct.)

21) *Hanging up persimmons–*
A cold, blustery wind
Turning bitterness
To sweetness

(Kyoto, Dec.)

22) *Minds of winter*
Glittering in skaters shoes
Music floats around

(Hirakata, Feb., 2018)

23) *Hidden behind swaying trees*
with fresh green leaves,
architect's monochrome building
standing still

(Oyamazaki, April)

24) *From Sewari's* cherry-trees*
Petals falling as a blizzard—
Our April Fools' Day stroll

(Kyoto, April)

*Located in Yawata, Kyoto, famous for cherry-blossoms.

25) *Half-hidden*
By the shrub of red sage–
Wild poppy sprouting

(Kyoto, May)

26) *To my sweating forehead*
A splash of waterfall–
Just halfway to the top

(Mt. Miwa, Nara, Oct.)

27) *The rock sanctuary:*
One family clapping hands in unison,
A lone woman staring faraway

(same as above)

28) *Fields of golden rice*
Ready for harvesting—
Ancient village, unchanged
(Asuka, Nara, Oct.)

29) *Lettuce fields gone—*
the Silicon Valley,
Covered with California smog
(San Jose, Calif., Nov.)

30) *University town,*
Once my alma mater—
Familiar scenes with different faces
(Berkeley, Calif., Nov.)

Following haiku I wrote were
previously published in the anthologies.

Persimmon, Hailstone Haiku Circle,
Kansai Japan, 2017

1) *An outburst of laughter*
fills the rakugo theater–*
New Year

*traditional Japanese 'stand up' comedy

(74)

2) *Late autumn stroll*
along the canal
different languages
floating by

(74)

3) *Snowy hilltop—*
below, a jewel-box town
glitters in the wind

(110)

Meltdown, Hailstone Haiku Circle,
Kansai Japan, 2013

4) *Cherry blossoms*
in mourning
victims
having vanished

(41)

5) *So this is the house*
of the late poet!
My neighborhood comes alive

(84)

6) *The Rocky Mountains–*
through prairies and sky
their crisp air streaming

(98)

7) *Sunlit beechwoods,*
twilit waves of silvergrass–
my Daisen souvenirs

(106)

8) *Arashiyama drizzle–*
cherry petals plastered
to the tram-car floor

(121)

9) *Laughter–*
children wrestling
with a giant trout

(157)

Afterword

Originally, I was not going to write the Afterword, but as I was reading a galley proof draft, I realized that since I wrote the Preface, I needed a section to wrap it up.

I chose to write this book in English, as I found I could express my emotions and feelings more honestly in the language. My English haiku together with essays and notes, are not translations from Japanese, but they came straight out from my heart.

The concept for the book materialized more concretely after I submitted about half of the drafts of essays and research notes. During this process, I realized that my consciousness had evolved. It was like writing letters to my past, and traveling from my birthplace, Oakland, California to where I reside now, Kyoto.

June was an extremely busy month for me due to three projects. First, I moderated a presentation on Kazuo Ishiguro at an academic conference. Secondly, I gave a lecture entitled “The Nikkei Experience: From WWⅡ until Today.” While getting ready for these tasks, simultaneously I have been reading and editing my drafts for this book.

Now that the first two projects have been completed and as I began to focus on this book more, I realized that this is more like my autobiography. The process of writing this book has made me aware once again that I am a product of two cultures and languages. It has also helped me recognize my two main interests: Nikkei studies and English haiku.

However, during the process of writing the book, I was often caught in a dilemma as my thoughts naturally shift between the two very different languages: the ambiguity of Japanese and preciseness of English. When I am struggling to find the right expression in English, I seem to find more accurate words in Japanese and vice versa. Being bilingual is convenient, but at the same time, it can be conflicting.

Compiling this book has been a difficult but an eye-opening experience for me. Nevertheless, as I said in Preface, I hope readers could identify with some of my ideas, though this does not mean everyone has to sympathize with them. Most of all, thank you for reading this book.

June 29, 2019

Kyoko Norma Nozaki

野﨑　京子

Acknowledgements

I would like to express my gratitude to the following:

Stephen Henry Gill (Tito), Kyoto University, for the reprinting of my nine haiku from *Persimmon* and *Meltdown,* in Chapter Ⅲ.

Richard Hodge, Shiga University of Medical Sciences, for reading and editing many of my articles and papers. I am indebted to him for his quick response in bringing my stories to life.

Akane Nozaki, UNESCO, Bangkok, for reviewing, editing and straightening up some statistics and facts.

Azusa Yano, Kyoto Sangyo University, for reading initial drafts.

Takashi Nakamura, Kyowa Printing Co., for being patient and informative about the publication of my works.

As always, I appreciate my husband of more than half a century, Mitsuhiro Nozaki, for his support and perseverance.

July, 2019

Kyoko Norma Nozaki

野﨑　京子

著 者 紹 介

野﨑京子（**Kyoko Norma Nozaki**）

アメリカ合衆国カリフォルニア生まれ。
カリフォルニア大学（バークレイ校）卒業
1989 年　S.I.T. 大学大学院言語教育修士（MA）
現在、京都産業大学文化学部名誉教授
研究分野：日系・アジア系アメリカ文学と文化・英語俳句

主な業績（著書、論文等）
――― 『強制収容とアイデンティティ・シフト　――日系二世・三世の「日本」と「アメリカ」』（世界思想社、2007 年）
――― 「公文書との出会いと記憶の再生　――ストーリーを生み出す歴史文書」『アジア系アメリカ文学を学ぶ人のために』（世界思想社、2011 年）
――― 「日系中南米人（JLA）補償に問われる「正義」『エスニシティを問い直す』（関西学院大学出版会、2012 年）
――― 「日系人強制収容再考　――フォートリンカーン（ビスマーク）抑留所訪問と州立大学講演を報じるメディアを通じて――『アメリカス研究』（天理大学アメリカス研究、No.18, 2013 年）
――― 研究ノート「日系アメリカ人作家が描く日本　――虚構の中の現実」（AALA Journal No.22, 2016 年）
――― 英語俳句　Persimmon（Hailstone Haiku Circle, 2017）
――― 英語俳句　Meltdown（Hailstone Haiku Circle, 2013）

KYOKO NORMA NOZAKI, Professor Emeritus of Cultural Studies in the Department of Intercultural Studies at Kyoto Sangyo University in Japan, was born in the United States and educated in both countries. She has numerous publications on Asian American Literature, the latest being “Japan as Portrayed by Japanese American Writers—Reality in Fiction.” (*AALA Journal,* No.22, 2016)

She authored three books, *Singing My Own Song* (Yamaguchi Shoten, 2000), *In-Between ---American Diaspora--- Three Short Stories by Jhumpa Lahiri* (in Japanese) (Yamaguchi Shoten, 2003) and *Internment and Identity Shift : Japan and America Through the Eyes of a Nisei and Sansei* (in Japanese) (Sekai Shisousha, 2007).

She co-authored many books in Japanese, including *For People Studying Asian American Literature* (Sekai Sisousha, 2011) and *Acculturation of Ethnic Groups* (Kwansai University Press, 2012).

English Haiku being her current interest, she contributed a number of pieces to *Meltdown* (2013) and *Persimmon* (2017), both by Hailstone Haiku Circle.

Bilingual Complex :
Collection of Essays and Notes Featuring English Haiku
バイリンガル・コンプレックス

2019 年 12 月 10 日　初版第 1 刷発行　定価はカバーに表記してあります

著　者　野﨑京子

発行者　中西　良

発行所　ナカニシヤ出版

〒606－8161
京都市左京区一乗寺木ノ本町 15 番地
Telephone　075－723－0111
Facsimile　075－723－0095
郵便振替　01030－0－13128

印刷・製本＝協和印刷

Printed in Japan.

ISBN 978－4－7795－1429－6　C1082